J

The Brooklyn Bridge

NEW YORK CITY'S GRACEFUL CONNECTION

Vicki Weiner

Children's Press®
A Division of Scholastic Inc.
New York / Toronto / London / Auckland / Sydney
Mexico City / New Delhi / Hong Kong
Danbury, Connecticut

Book Design: Michelle Innes and Erica Clendening
Contributing Editor: M. Pitt
Photo Credits: Cover © Alan Schein Photography/Corbis; p. 4 The Phelps
Stokes Collection, Miriam and Ira D. Wallach Division of Art, Prints and
Photographs, The New York Public Library, Astor, Lenox and Tilden
Foundations; pp. 6–7, 11, 18 © Corbis; p. 8 New-York Historical
Society/Bridgeman Art Library; pp. 11 (inset), 36 Library of Congress, Prints
and Photographs Division; p. 14 © Underwood and Underwood/Corbis; p. 16
Library of Congress, Prints and Photographs Division, HAER, NY, 31-NEYO, 90;
p. 20 © AP/Wide World Photos; pp. 22, 32 © Hulton/Archive/Getty Images;
p. 25 The Stapleton Collection/Bridgeman Art Library; pp. 26, 30 ©
Bettmann/Corbis; p. 35 © Gary Braasch/Corbis; p. 39 © Museum of the City
of New York/Corbis; pp. 40–41 © James Rudnick/Corbis

Library of Congress Cataloging-in-Publication Data

Weiner, Vicki.
    The Brooklyn Bridge : New York City's graceful connection / by Vicki
Weiner.
    p. cm.—(Architectural wonders)
    Summary: Describes the construction of the Brooklyn Bridge, from its
conception by John Roebling in 1852 through many setbacks to its final
completion under the direction of his son, Washington, in 1883.
    ISBN 0-516-24080-3 (lib. bdg.)—ISBN 0-516-25905-9 (pbk.)
    1. Brooklyn Bridge (New York, N.Y.)—History—Juvenile literature. 2.
New York (N.Y.)—Buildings, structures, etc.—Juvenile literature. [1.
Brooklyn Bridge (New York, N.Y.)—History. 2. Bridges—Design and
construction.] I. Title. II. Series.

TG25.N53W48 2003
624'.5'097471—dc21

                                                    2003010308

    1 2 3 4 5 6 7 8 9 10 R 13 12 11 10 09 08 07 06 05 04

Contents

Introduction 4

Before the Bridge 8

Death of a Dreamer 16

Bridging the Gap 22

Two Great Cities Joined 32

New Words 42

For Further Reading 44

Resources 45

Index 47

About the Author 48

Introduction

Brooklyn and Manhattan stand only half a mile apart. In the 1850s that distance seemed much more vast than it does today.

Imagine you live in Brooklyn, New York. It's a bitterly cold winter morning in the 1850s. A frozen East River separates you from the city of New York, where you go to school. (At this time, Brooklyn was a separate city from the city of New York.) You stand in line at the Fulton Ferry house, waiting for a boat to take you across. Hundreds of other people also need to cross the choppy waters. However, you're soon told the ferryboats can't make the trip today. Floating chunks of ice make crossing the river too dangerous.

Traveling across the East River during this time was very hard. The trip could only be made by boat. Although the journey was only half a mile long (.8 kilometers), it could be deadly. Boats bobbed along the choppy waters. On a stormy or foggy day, boats often crashed into each other. The water is also very deep and has dangerous currents.

One day in 1852, engineer John Augustus Roebling and his son, Washington, were stuck on a ferry to Brooklyn. The ferry got caught between huge chunks of ice. John Roebling stood on the deck, looking at the other stranded boats. He watched men attempt to walk across frozen sections of river. With every step, they risked their lives.

Clearly, the East River needed a bridge that stretched from shore to shore. John Roebling knew that designing and building this bridge would be

Before the Brooklyn Bridge was built, crossing the East River could be a dangerous affair.

a huge challenge. It would have to be much longer than any bridge in the world. It would also have to allow tall ships to pass underneath—yet be strong enough to support a roadway. That day, John Roebling began to put his vision to work. His effort and imagination would help create New York's world-famous Brooklyn Bridge.

chapter one

Before the Bridge

John Roebling longed to use his talents as an engineer in the United States. Once he constructed his famous iron wire cable, he got his chance.

John Roebling was a native of Germany. After studying engineering at his country's finest technical school, he came to the United States. It was 1831. Roebling was twenty-five years old. He wanted to put his skills and education to work. He and a group of fellow Germans purchased a large plot of land in Pennsylvania. The group built houses, stores, and churches on the land. They called their new farming town Saxonburg.

Roebling found the farmer's life too quiet, though. He told his son, Washington, that he longed to "employ science to useful purpose." In the early 1840s, Roebling got his first chance to do just that. He knew a new type of rope called wire cable was being used in Europe. It was made from iron wires. These wires were twisted together to form a long strand. Roebling made the first iron wire cable in the United States.

At first, people doubted that Roebling's cable could work better than rope. Once tested it, though, they were amazed. The iron cable was thinner, stronger, and longer lasting than ordinary rope. Soon, delighted business owners were snatching up Roebling's iron cables. They used the cables to haul heavy loads over Pennsylvania's Allegheny Mountains.

A Better Bridge

Roebling's cable helped him create the modern suspension bridge. A suspension bridge spans a wide body of water. Ancient bridges were held up by rope made from hemp. Today's bridges are held up by thick metal cables. The cables are attached to two strong towers, made of stone, steel, or iron. These towers hold the bridge in place. The roadway is suspended, or held up, by the cable.

In 1861 the American Civil War began. John's son, Washington, served in the Union Army. He even fought in the battle at Gettysburg. As a colonel, he built temporary suspension bridges using his father's ideas. Washington soon became his father's chief engineer.

Together, father and son built many suspension bridges. One of their most famous works was built in Cincinnati, Ohio. The Cincinnati Bridge spanned the Ohio River. At the time, in 1872, it was the largest suspension bridge ever seen. It was a triumph of engineering skills. Yet both father and son knew that harder work lay ahead. John Roebling never rested. He was an ambitious, driven man. Once he got an idea for a new bridge, he never forgot it.

Many people in New York doubted that a bridge suspended by wire rope would work. By building his first masterpiece, the Cincinnati Bridge (above), John Roebling proved his doubters wrong.

Cross-section of a Caisson

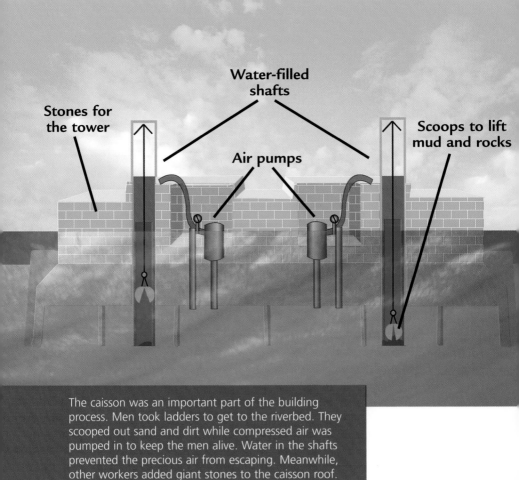

Water-filled shafts

Stones for the tower

Air pumps

Scoops to lift mud and rocks

The caisson was an important part of the building process. Men took ladders to get to the riverbed. They scooped out sand and dirt while compressed air was pumped in to keep the men alive. Water in the shafts prevented the precious air from escaping. Meanwhile, other workers added giant stones to the caisson roof.

Foundations for Success

John Roebling knew that his greatest idea—a bridge stretching from New York to Brooklyn—would be his greatest challenge, too. The two towers securing the wire cable suspension system would have to be tall and steady. Roebling's plan called for each tower to be a whopping 268 feet (81.7 meters) tall. The towers would be placed in the water just off each shore. They would rest on foundations, or bases, dug deeply into the riverbed.

Washington Roebling decided these towers should be built on caissons. A caisson is a large box made of wood and iron. It is closed on all sides, except the bottom. A caisson's walls are very strong, although its inside chamber is hollow.

The Roeblings planned on sinking the caissons into the East River. Each caisson would weigh 3,000 tons (2,721.6 metric tons). The rim of its open bottom would rest on the riverbed. Air would need to be constantly pumped into the caisson. Air pressure would keep the river water out.

Men would climb ladders to get in and out of the caisson. These ladders would provide access to the riverbed. There, workers would shovel and scoop out the riverbed's sand and dirt. While in the chamber, they would be protected from the river by a pocket of compressed air. The air would also allow them to breathe while they worked. Meanwhile, other men would work on top of the caisson. These workers

This diver is about to work inside a caisson. Many men who worked on the Brooklyn Bridge suffered from an illness that affected their breathing and their arms and legs due to the work they did in similar caissons.

would be building the tower on the caisson's roof with heavy stones.

As the digging continued below, and the tower was being built above, the caisson would sink deeper into the riverbed. Eventually, it would hit a hard surface under the sand. This surface, called bedrock, would be the foundation for the caissons and the towers. The caisson would then be filled in with concrete.

Around that time, another bridge designer, James Eads, was building a bridge in St. Louis, Missouri. He also used caissons to set his bridge's foundations in place. However, a problem arose. Some of Eads's workers had fallen prey to a mysterious illness after leaving the caisson. One worker finished his shift feeling fine. Minutes later, struggling for breath, he was dead. This worker's tragic death alerted the Roeblings to the dangers that might arise as they built the bridge.

chapter two

Death of a Dreamer

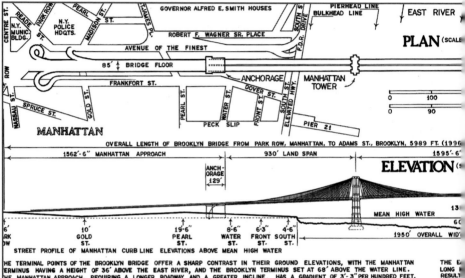

GOVERNOR ALFRED E. SMITH HOUSES   PIERHEAD LINE   EAST RIVER
BULKHEAD LINE
READE ST. PARK ROW PEARL ST. THAMES PL. SO. ST. SOUTH DRIVE
N.Y. MUNIC. BLDG. N.Y. POLICE HDQTS. MADISON ST. ROBERT F. WAGNER SR. PLACE F.D.R. DRIVE
CENTRE ST. AVENUE OF THE FINEST
ROW 85' ↕ BRIDGE FLOOR   ANCHORAGE   MANHATTAN TOWER **PLAN** (SCALE
FRANKFORT ST. DOVER ST. ELEVATED HWY.
NASSAU ST. SPRUCE ST. GOLD ST. PEARL ST. WATER ST. FRONT ST. SOUTH ST. 0 100
MANHATTAN   PECK SLIP   PIER 21 0 90

OVERALL LENGTH OF BROOKLYN BRIDGE FROM PARK ROW, MANHATTAN, TO ADAMS ST., BROOKLYN, 5989 FT. (1996

| 1562'-6" MANHATTAN APPROACH | 930' LAND SPAN | 1595'-6" |

ANCH-ORAGE 129' **ELEVATION** (S

MEAN HIGH WATER   13

6'   10'   19'-6"   8'-6"   6'-3"   4'-6"   60
RK GOLD PEARL WATER FRONT SOUTH 1950' OVERALL WID
DW ST. ST. ST. ST. ST.

STREET PROFILE OF MANHATTAN CURB LINE ELEVATIONS ABOVE MEAN HIGH WATER

HE TERMINAL POINTS OF THE BROOKLYN BRIDGE OFFER A SHARP CONTRAST IN THEIR GROUND ELEVATIONS, WITH THE MANHATTAN
TERMINUS HAVING A HEIGHT OF 36' ABOVE THE EAST RIVER, AND THE BROOKLYN TERMINUS SET AT 68' ABOVE THE WATER LINE.
HE MANHATTAN APPROACH, REQUIRING A LONGER ROADWAY AND A GREATER INCLINE, HAS A GRADIENT OF 3'-3" PER HUNDRED FEET.
HE BROOKLYN APPROACH REQUIRES A GRADIENT OF ONLY 1'-9" PER HUNDRED FEET.

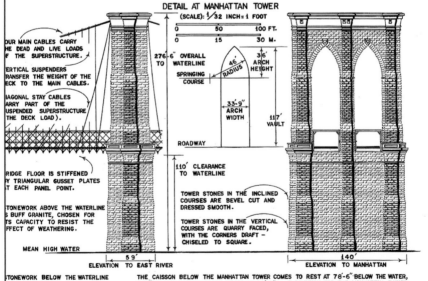

DETAIL AT MANHATTAN TOWER
(SCALE): 1/32 INCH= 1 FOOT
0 .... 50 .... 100 FT.
0 ...... 15 ...... 30 M.

OUR MAIN CABLES CARRY
HE DEAD AND LIVE LOADS
F THE SUPERSTRUCTURE.

ERTICAL SUSPENDERS
RANSFER THE WEIGHT OF THE
ECK TO THE MAIN CABLES.

IAGONAL STAY CABLES
ARRY PART OF THE
USPENDED SUPERSTRUCTURE
THE DECK LOAD).

RIDGE FLOOR IS STIFFENED
Y TRIANGULAR GUSSET PLATES
T EACH PANEL POINT.

TONEWORK ABOVE THE WATERLINE
S BUFF GRANITE, CHOSEN FOR
TS CAPACITY TO RESIST THE
FFECT OF WEATHERING.

MEAN HIGH WATER

276'-6" OVERALL
TO WATERLINE
SPRINGING COURSE
46' RADIUS
36' ARCH HEIGHT
33'-9" ARCH WIDTH
117' VAULT
ROADWAY
110' CLEARANCE TO WATERLINE

TOWER STONES IN THE INCLINED
COURSES ARE BEVEL CUT AND
DRESSED SMOOTH.

TOWER STONES IN THE VERTICAL
COURSES ARE QUARRY FACED,
WITH THE CORNERS DRAFT -
CHISELED TO SQUARE.

59' ELEVATION TO EAST RIVER   140' ELEVATION TO MANHATTAN

TONEWORK BELOW THE WATERLINE   THE CAISSON BELOW THE MANHATTAN TOWER COMES TO REST AT 78'-6" BELOW THE WATER,
S BLUE LIMESTONE, CHOSEN FOR   AND THE BROOKLYN CAISSON RESTS AT 44'-6". EXCAVATION FOR THE MANHATTAN TOWER
TS CAPACITY TO ABSORB ITS OWN   WAS HALTED IN 1872 WHEN THE TOLL FROM THE "CAISSON DISEASE" ROSE TO 5 DEAD AND 110

THE E
LONG
RESULT
CHANGE

THE B
BORN
HE RE
POLYTE
PRUSS
AMERIC
COMMI
FALLS,
ENGINE
SURVE
INJURE
DIED
BY HI
HAVING
WAS
DEATH
TRAINI
TECHN
1861
AND
CHANC
STAFF,
PROJE
THAT

THE F
PIERH
CAISS
OPEN
LONG,
DRIVE
TO TH
TOWE
WAS
EXCAV
TO C
AIR P
AS T
BEDRO
AND

John Roebling first presented his plan for the Brooklyn Bridge in 1867. His idea pleased many. Others thought Roebling's bridge seemed unnecessary. New Yorkers didn't go frequently to Brooklyn. To them, the project was a waste of money. On the other hand, Brooklyn's residents were in favor of a bridge. Brooklyn was growing fast as a city. Its residents needed an easier way to travel to New York for work, school, shopping, and entertainment.

The Cold, Hard Truth

Public opinion was divided. However, the terrible winter of 1866–67 swayed many city leaders' minds. Icy conditions along the East River froze ferry service for days on end. This convinced Brooklyn's mayor that the city couldn't continue to grow without a bridge. Meanwhile, New Yorkers were warming to the idea, too. They knew that Brooklyn was booming. Still, it remained a cheaper and less crowded city than New York. It would be wonderful to have easy access to Brooklyn's charms. On April 16, 1867, New York's legislature created the New York Bridge Company. The company would be dedicated to Roebling's dream—constructing a bridge over the East River. John Roebling was asked to be the bridge's designer.

These modern drawings of the bridge's Gothic towers are based on Roebling's original sketches. The names of modern-day streets and buildings can be seen at the top of the drawing.

Roebling worked hard to make his vision come alive for others. Once the public saw what the bridge could mean to them, they grew excited.

Tragedy Strikes

Excitement about the bridge swelled. It was going to be unlike any structure seen before. Its length would measure 1,596 feet (486 m) from tower to tower. This would make it one-and-a-half times longer than the Cincinnati Bridge. The Brooklyn Bridge's towers would feature 117-foot-high (35.7 m) Gothic arches. Horse and carriage riders would use outer lanes across the span. Trains would travel across the bridge's inner lanes. A special walkway, called a promenade, would be built above the roadways.

Pedestrians, or people walking, would stroll across the promenade and be treated to magnificent views of the city.

Everyone knew the completed bridge would be beautiful. However, many worried it would not be safe. Roebling invited a group of experts to study his plans. These experts were impressed with Roebling's vision. Finally, in 1869, all their questions were answered. The two cities gave their final approvals.

Mere days later, John Roebling stood at the Fulton Ferry landing, speaking with Washington. They were discussing where the Brooklyn tower should be placed. Suddenly, a ferry bumped into the dock. John Roebling's right foot was crushed in the impact. He fell over in pain. In the weeks that followed, the pain grew worse. Roebling's doctor was forced to amputate, or cut off, his toes. Soon after, an infection called tetanus set in. It caused Roebling's facial muscles to stiffen. His jaw nearly froze shut. Eventually, he went into a coma, or deep state of unconsciousness. On July 22, 1869, John Roebling died.

Passing the Torch

People remembered an old superstition that a safe bridge demanded a human life. Everyone was in

Washington Roebling eventually had 1,100 men working for him on the Brooklyn Bridge. In the days right after his father died, however, few people knew whether he would be able to continue John Roebling's dream.

shock, though, that the life taken was John Roebling's. Now that the dreamer had died, would his dream die with him?

A month later, the New York Bridge Company asked Washington Roebling to take his father's place. It was an obvious choice. Washington had worked closely with John on bridge projects. He knew all there was to know about the wire cable system.

Still, Washington was different than his father in many ways. At thirty-two years old, he was still a young engineer. He was not as experienced or confident as his father. However, Washington shared one crucial thing with his father—a desire to see Brooklyn and New York linked. Like his father, Washington longed to see the bridge built. He accepted the challenge of being the chief engineer.

There was much to do before construction could start. Washington hired a team of engineers to assist him. They ordered equipment, looked at stone samples, and began hiring builders. Thanks to his son, John Roebling's awesome dream had been set back in motion.

chapter three

Bridging the Gap

Day after day, the men worked steadily under Roebling's guidance. With each block, they were growing closer to bringing two cities together.

Washington had to get right to work building the caissons. They would create a safe, airtight space for the workers to dig underwater. The first caisson was built in a shipyard on the Brooklyn waterfront. It was finished in March 1870. For the next three months, the crew prepared the Brooklyn tower site. Meanwhile, the caisson bobbed in the water near the shipyard. The air pumped into the caisson's hollow chamber made it float like an enormous, upside-down boat.

In May, a barge carried the caisson to its proper spot on the river. The spot was at the Fulton Ferry landing—the same place where John Roebling's foot had been crushed. Workers sank the caisson to the riverbed. The men climbed down air shafts to begin digging out the river bottom. Dirt, rock, and sand were dumped into a shallow pool of water. Then a clamlike bucket, called a clam-digger, grabbed the debris. The clam-digger was sent up a water shaft to the caisson's roof. Workers on the roof unloaded the clam-digger and sent it back down the shaft. Inch by inch, the caisson sank deeper into the riverbed.

The conditions inside the caisson were terrible. It was like being in a dark, damp cave. Men found it somewhat difficult to breathe. The compressed air being pumped in made voices and noises sound very strange. Candles, lanterns, and gas burners inside the chamber kept temperatures terribly hot.

Other men worked on top of the caisson, building the tower. They set the huge limestone blocks into place on the caisson's roof. Each layer built the tower up, and sank the caisson deeper. Slowly, the Brooklyn tower was taking shape.

Danger and Disease

Washington Roebling lived near the Brooklyn waterfront with his wife, Emily, and their son, John. Washington spent many hours inside the caisson, working alongside his men. He constantly worried about the conditions inside the chamber. The use of compressed air, burning candles, and explosives made it very likely that a fire would break out. In December 1870, a fire did start. The compressed air made the fire nearly smokeless, and almost invisible. Washington stayed in the caisson all night trying to put it out. For a while, the workers believed that the danger was over. Soon, though, fire was discovered again. The fact that the flames were invisible made it nearly impossible for the men to know whether the fire was still blazing. Washington ordered his engineers to turn off the compressed air. Then he had them flood the caisson with water. At last, the blaze was put out.

While workers above the caisson piled rocks on top of one another, other men dug deep beneath the river. They used sledgehammers to break apart the bigger boulders.

Most people agreed that the bridge's two towers were magnificent. Yet what makes the bridge work are the thick iron cables shown here.

Other Dangers

Sometimes, when the tide rose or a large ship went by the work site, the caisson became unsettled. Its position on the river floor would shift, forcing a big bubble of air to escape from underneath the caisson. The huge air bubble would force water, sand, and fish up out of the river. This was known as a blowout. The blowouts made a roaring sound as the compressed air escaped high into the air above the river. People watching from the shore

The bends are caused by nitrogen bubbles that form in the blood as a person goes from compressed air to normal air. The cure is to leave the compressed air very slowly.

could see dramatic waterspouts shooting out. The blowouts were scary, but didn't do much damage.

Blasted by the Bends

The caisson sank farther each day, getting closer to the solid bedrock. The men were slowly getting used to spending time in the compressed air. However, many of them were beginning to feel sick when they came out of the chamber. Their illness was known as caisson disease, or the bends. Arm pains, leg pains, dizziness, and vomiting plagued the workers. No one was quite sure what was causing the bends, or how to stop it.

The bends were unpleasant. For some men, the disease even caused brief paralysis. For the most part, though, their symptoms were mild.

Washington's own attacks were mild, too. However, the disease would later prove far more serious, as the men worked inside the New York caisson.

The Disease Digs In

The Brooklyn caisson was finally finished in March 1871. It rested on bedrock nearly 45 feet (13.7 m) below the East River. Workers filled its chamber with concrete, making it a very solid foundation for the Brooklyn tower.

Completing the caisson on the Brooklyn side taught Washington valuable lessons. He was able to put these lessons to good use when beginning work on the New York caisson. Washington made this caisson a safer, more pleasant workplace. However, the river floor on the New York side was much sandier than on the Brooklyn side. The bedrock was farther down. This caisson would need to be sunk nearly twice as deep.

As the New York caisson sank lower, cases of the bends increased. Symptoms were much more severe, and attacks lasted longer. When the New York caisson was more than 60 feet (18.3 m) under the river, two workers died from the disease. Washington was growing sicker himself. He suffered sharp pains in his arms and legs, as well as fainting spells. He hired a doctor to look after his men. The doctor didn't really understand how to prevent the bends, though. In the 1870s the importance of slowly coming out of the compressed air wasn't known.

In May 1872 the caisson reached a depth of 78 feet, 6 inches (23.9 m). Roebling ordered the men to stop digging. He thought this depth would provide a fine foundation. However, the caisson had not quite reached the bedrock, so Washington was taking a huge risk.

Window Watching

By December a weakened Washington Roebling ordered the work on the two towers stopped due to harsh winter weather. He and Emily traveled to Germany to look for a cure for the bends. None was found. After a few months, the couple came back to America. Work started again on the towers.

With Emily's constant help, Washington wrote letters every day to the engineers at the site. He gave advice. He also spent countless hours working out the design for the bridge anchorages. This is where

Washington Roebling's devotion to the Brooklyn Bridge took a huge toll on his health. However, he took heart in the fact that he could watch the bridge's progress from his home.

the suspension cables coming off the towers would be anchored onto dry land.

Washington continued fighting his illness. He and Emily set up an office in their Brooklyn home. The rising towers of the bridge could be seen from the house. Washington used field glasses to watch the activities on the building site. Emily became a crucial part of the building team. She visited the site every day. She delivered her husband's letters and drawings. She returned with the engineers' questions. At home, she read to Washington constantly—newspaper articles, letters from the New York Bridge Company—anything that concerned the Brooklyn Bridge. Together, Washington and Emily oversaw the placement of each stone.

chapter four

Two Great Cities Joined

One month after the one hundredth birthday of the United States, Frank Farrington glided from one tower to the next. It's safe to say that his journey was more unusual than the one most Brooklyn Bridge travelers take!

By July 1876 the Brooklyn Bridge's towers were complete. They wound up standing taller than John Roebling had predicted—276 feet, 6 inches (84.3 m) above the water. It was a proud period in history. With the Civil War over, the nation was united once again. Americans were celebrating their nation's one hundredth birthday. Achievements in art and science were springing up everywhere. Thomas Edison was hard at work developing the electric light. Author Mark Twain was hard at work writing his novel *Huckleberry Finn*. The two towers were another sign of the United States's growth. They were also beautiful, just as John Roebling had intended them to be. His plan for the bridge to be capped by graceful Gothic arches was successful. The bridge's strength was certainly matched by its beauty.

In August 1876 thousands of amazed spectators were treated to a wild sight. Master mechanic Frank Farrington became the first man to travel across the bridge. He glided across the river on a small hanging seat, which was attached to a single cable.

The bridge was still far from completion, however. It would take seven more years before the public could make its journey across the river. Some workers were busy spinning cable. They were wrapping over 14,000 miles (22,530 km) of steel wire together to form the bridge's four main cables. Another group

Most men working in the caissons earned about two dollars a day.

of workers strung suspender cables downward from the top of the main cables. The suspender cables were attached to the roadways' steel floor beams. They supported the bridge's road and walkways. Still other workers wove in special steel wire cables called diagonal stays. While the diagonal stays weren't in John Roebling's original design, he surely would have approved. The stays strengthened the bridge and gave it its famous, weblike beauty.

The Final Push

Washington Roebling was still very sick. Emily spent all of her waking hours writing his instructions and delivering them to the site. She met with the Bridge Company and inspected the work. The couple formed an amazing partnership. Some people grumbled that a woman shouldn't be given such

One of Washington Roebling's personal additions was the cables called diagonal stays. The stays make the bridge seem to be connected by some sort of gleaming, enormous spiderweb.

Few people believed Emily Roebling could help fill her husband's shoes after he became sick. A few years later, even fewer people doubted Emily's strength and wisdom.

power. Emily rose to the occasion, though. Without her courage and leadership, the bridge's progress might have been halted.

Instead, it continued. Roads leading to the bridge in Brooklyn and New York were built. Train stations at each end of the bridge were finished. For a short time, pedestrians were allowed to walk across a temporary footbridge.

Around noon on June 14, 1878, a terrible accident happened. A wire strand snapped and killed two workers. Other workers were bloody and groaning but still alive. The public became nervous. Twenty-one men, including John Roebling, had now died working on the Brooklyn Bridge. Its construction was now in its fourteenth year. Would it claim more lives? Would it be safe? Would it ever be finished?

BUILDING BLOCKS

In 1898, Brooklyn and New York merged into one great city.

A Completed Dream

On May 24, 1883, one of the nation's grandest celebrations kicked off in style. The Brooklyn Bridge was finally complete. United States President Chester Arthur and New York Governor Grover Cleveland attended the festivities. The president led a march across the bridge. Thousands followed behind him while a band played patriotic songs. When the president reached the Brooklyn tower, Emily Roebling and the mayor of Brooklyn were there to greet him. The Roeblings held a big reception at their house. Their great sacrifice had paid off.

About 150,000 people traveled across the bridge that day. After sunset, fireworks were shot into the clear night sky. The red, blue, and yellow streams of light fell in soft arcs all around the bridge. Tens of thousands of people watched from streets and rooftops. Others gazed up from boats. When the fireworks finished, a long row of electric lights lit the bridge. At last, John Roebling's dream had come true. Its cost was truly great—more than 15 million dollars, and far worse, twenty-one human lives.

Still Standing Tall

Within a year of opening, over 37,000 people were crossing the Brooklyn Bridge each day. Most crossed by carriage or on the bridge train. The bridge's fame as the longest suspension bridge in the world lasted

After enduring illness and uncertainty, Washington and Emily Roebling must have been overjoyed to witness the opening ceremony of their great achievement.

until 1903, when the Williamsburg Bridge was constructed nearby. It was about 5 feet (1.5 m) longer than the Brooklyn Bridge, and also hung with Roebling wire cables.

However, the Brooklyn Bridge remains many New Yorkers' most beloved bridge. Today, more than 160,000 people use it to cross the East River each day. In the 1940s the bridge was transformed to allow a new form of travel—automobiles. The train tracks were removed at this time. The promenade above the roadway is still there, though. It's a great way to take in the wonderful views of the New York skyline.

In a city filled with glorious sights, one of the greatest and most enduring is the Brooklyn Bridge.

The Roeblings might not have guessed that sky-scrapers would someday rise far above the bridge's towers. They would surely be proud, however, to see that the Gothic arches have lasted over one hundred years. The Brooklyn Bridge remains an amazing feat of engineering and willpower. It also remains one of the true symbols of New York City.

41

New Words

anchorages (**ang**-kur-ij-iz) objects built on land that secure the cables of a suspension bridge

bedrock (**bed**-rok) the solid layer of rock under the soil and loose rock

cable (**kay**-buhl) a thick wire or rope

caisson (**kay**-suhn) a watertight chamber used in construction work underwater

caisson disease (**kay**-suhn duh-**zeez**) a painful, sometimes fatal disease caused by the release of gas bubbles in tissue upon a too rapid decrease in air pressure after a stay in a compressed atmosphere

chamber (**chaym**-bur) a large room

compressed (kuhm-**pressd**) pressed into a smaller space

diagonal stays (dye-**ag**-uh-nuhl **stayz**) wires strung on an angle from the main cables of a bridge that help to brace vertical wires

New Words

engineer (en-juh-**nihr**) someone who is trained to design and build machines, vehicles, bridges, roads, or other structures

ferry (**fer**-ee) a boat or ship that regularly carries people across a stretch of water

Gothic arches (**goth**-ic **arch**-iz) pointed arches; a style of arches found in the twelfth to sixteenth centuries in Europe

hemp (**hemp**) a plant whose fibers are used to make rope

span (**span**) the length from one end to the other of something, such as a bridge

suspension bridge (suh-**spen**-shuhn **brij**) a bridge hung from cables or chains strung from towers

For Further Reading

Adkins, Jan E. *Bridges: From My Side to Yours*. Brookfield, CT: Millbrook Press, 2002.

Curlee, Lynn. *Brooklyn Bridge*. New York: Atheneum Books for Young Readers, 2001.

Kent, Zachary. *The Story of the Brooklyn Bridge*. Danbury, CT: Children's Press, 1988.

Mann, Elizabeth B. *The Brooklyn Bridge*. New York: Mikaya Press, 1996.

Pascoe, Elaine. *The Brooklyn Bridge*. Farmington Hills, MI: Gale Group, 1999.

Resources

Organizations

The New-York Historical Society
2 West 77th Street
New York, NY 10024
Phone: (212) 873-3400
www.nyhistory.org

Museum of the City of New York
1220 Fifth Avenue
New York, NY 10029
Phone: (212) 534-1672
www.mcny.org

Brooklyn Historical Society
45 Main Street, Suite 617
Brooklyn, NY 11201
Phone: (718) 222-4111
www.brooklynhistory.org

Brooklyn Heights Association
55 Pierrepont Street
Brooklyn, NY 11201
Phone: (718) 858-9193

Resources

Video

Brooklyn Bridge. Director: Ken Burns, 1982. Warner Home Video.

Web Sites

PBS Kids: Learning Adventures in Citizenship
www.pbs.org/wnet/newyork/laic/episode3/topic1/ e3_topic1.html
This site walks you through the building of the bridge.

ASCE History and Heritage of Civil Engineering
www.asce.org/history/brdg_brooklyn.html
This site has links to information about the Roeblings. It also has a map of the Brooklyn Bridge with points you can click on for a virtual tour.

Bridge Engineering Bookstore
www.bridgesite.com/BookStore.htm
This site follows in the Roeblings' footsteps and features books about building bridges.

Index

A

anchorages, 29

B

bedrock, 15, 27–29
blowout, 27

C

cable, 9–10, 12, 21, 31, 33–34, 39
caisson, 12–13, 15, 23–24, 26–29
caisson disease (the bends), 27–29
chamber, 13, 23–24, 27–28
Cincinnati Bridge, 10
compressed, 13, 23–24, 27, 29

D

diagonal stays, 34

E

East River, 5, 13, 17, 28, 40
engineer, 5, 10, 21, 24, 29, 31

F

ferry, 5, 17, 19, 23
Fulton Ferry, 5, 19, 23

G

Gothic arches, 18, 33, 41

H

hemp, 10

N

New York Bridge Company, 17, 21, 31

P

pedestrians, 19, 36
promenade, 18–19

Index

R

Roebling, Emily, 24, 29, 31, 34, 36–37

Roebling, John Augustus, 5, 7, 9–10, 12–13, 15, 17, 19, 21, 23, 33–34, 37–38, 41

Roebling, Washington, 9–10, 13, 15, 19, 21, 23–24, 28–29, 31, 34

S

span, 10, 18

suspension bridge, 10, 38

T

tower, 10, 12–13, 15, 18–19, 23–24, 28–29, 31, 33, 37, 41

W

wire cable suspension system, 12

About the Author

Vicki Weiner lives in Brooklyn, a short walk from the Brooklyn Bridge. She first came to know and love the bridge in graduate school when she studied the history of New York City. Vicki works in the field of historic preservation, which is concerned with saving buildings, parks, bridges, and art. She is married to an architect and has a four-year-old son.